2017.

To

My Dearest Friend

Maureen Mary!

with

love & best

Wishes

Catrin

x

CORNISH AND SUSSEX RECOLLECTIONS IN
TEXTILE ART

CATRIN EDWARDS-JONES

COUNTRY BOOKS

Published by Country Books
Courtyard Cottage, Little Longstone, Bakewell, Derbyshire DE45 1NN
Tel: 01629 640670
e-mail: dickrichardson@country-books.co.uk
www.countrybooks.biz

ISBN 978-1-910489-36-9

Printed and bound in England by 4dge Ltd, Hockley, Essex. Tel: 01702 200243

DEDICATION

For Marrietta Triffitt, Hilda Mositano, Christa Hamplin and Marhietta Hale

CONTENTS

INTRODUCTION

The Quilters guild of Britain was formed in 1979 with a founding membership of 300, Catrin Edwards-Jones was the 11TH member to join the guild.

In the early 1980's, Catrin, a resident in Brighton, became the founder of The Sussex Quilters', with its membership of twelve very enthusiastic needle women. They all met weekly for enjoyable quilting sessions in each other's homes; learning many patchwork, applique and quilting methods. After a while it was decided to create a large 'block' patchwork hanging; depicting Brighton and its surroundings. A successful television programme resulted, covering the making of the Sussex hanging and the finished work.

Further quilting sessions, due to an increase in membership after the exposure on television, were later held in a small hall in Southwick on the outskirts of Brighton.

On leaving Brighton to open a textile studio in St. Ives, Cornwall, Catrin left the running in the capable hands of Wyn, a founder member of the Sussex Quilters'.

THE ST. IVES QUILTERS'

It had happened over night!

In 1985 Catrin Edwards-Jones had not long moved to St. Ives in Cornwall from her Brighton home in East Sussex before she opened a Textile Studio there. Her newly acquired studio was situated in St. Ives Bunker's Hill coverted from a cellar that had been used for pressing salted pilchards into wooden barrels, to a small working studio displaying and selling Catrin's textile pictures, hangings and speciality designs in creative textile art.

Not long after her opening, a local hotelier and a quilter, Marriette, called into her studio early in the New Year.

"Catrin, would you consider giving a slide talk on Patchwork and Quilting in our hotel during the quiet period – maybe, early in the New

Year?" Catrin nodded, with an 'alright' acknowledgement.

The snow-beaten day arrived, there were no hopes of much attendance, but to Marriette and Catrin's utter amazement over fifty enthusiastic people arrived from all parts of the county. They were invited in with a glass of wine, followed at half time with a cup of coffee. Pencil and paper had been left in the hotel's foyer. Perhaps someone present wished to join a suggested local quilting group? Much to Catrin's surprise, over twenty names came forward and –

The St. Ives Quilters' was born.

A very interesting fun-loving group of local ladies began to join Catrin in her studio with the aim of creating something worthy of St. Ives. Possibly, a putting together of a hanging in appliqued patchwork and quilting, of their favourite views of St. Ives as seen from their homes. Photographs of their individual choices arrived on the second meeting and were transformed into personalised twelve inch textile squares each appliqued and quilted. Within twelve months the hanging was near completion, applied and quilted showing quite unusual views of St. Ives. It was decided to give the sixteen block hanging a surrounding, in tones of blue, as the town was, more or less, surrounded by the sea: within twelve months their work was nearing completion.

The Quilters' Guild was due to have their annual A.G.M. in Devon – the occasion included a South West Competition. Their suggested specification was a quilted hanging representing 'The Sea', Our St. Ives ladies had to finish their quilt for the occasion.

Just imagine how delighted they were on receiving First Prize!

Following this, the Quilt was lent to the St. Ives' Parish Church, on the harbour, in order to boost the church funds for the restoration of a stained glass window above the main entrance into the church.

For the next season, the quilt created a great deal of interest while on display in the St. Ives' Museum during summer months.

While the St. Ives' hanging was on show during an exhibition of Quilts in Truro Museum the following year, two St. Ives' doctors, following a visit to the exhibition, put in a request for the hanging to be donated on a permanent loan to the newly refurbished Medical Centre in St. Ives.

The St. Ives Quilters' interesting creation hangs in the main reception area of the Medical Centre and is constantly enjoyed by their patients as they come and go.

ILLUSTRATIONS

PART THREE – SUSSEX

SUSSEX

PART ONE
1951-1985

Depicted mostly in Textile Art

SUSSEX RECOLLECTIONS

CHERRY TREE COTTAGE 1768 – 1960

A lovely small villa nestling in a third of an acre and privately enclosed by a six foot high Sussex wall. Cherry Tree Cottage was situated on the outskirts of a West Sussex coastal town and had been given to the owners as a wedding present in 1951.

Cherry Tree Cottage was tragically demolished by the local district council in 1962 so as to make way for a roundabout to ease the flow of traffic travelling towards London.

Here are memories of Cherry Tree Cottage; a photograph, textile art, painting, cushion and a miniature in wood of the old Georgian home.

A framed sampler of Cherry Tree Cottage, created in 1956 on pale blue cotton fabric; house, roof and side wall appliqued and finalised in various forms of hand embroidery.

FACING PAGE ABOVE:
Cherry Tree Cottage
– oil on canvas

FACING PAGE BELOW:
Cherry Tree Cottage
– a cushion
Wool – hand-knitting, crochet and embroidery

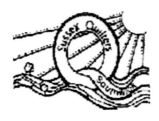

THE SUSSEX QUILTERS'

The Sussex Quilters' was established by Catrin in the 1980's (and is still going strong in 2016.) Members met regularly in each other's homes to create various patchwork pieces – bed, table and cushion covers in English and American patchwork. This large 'Block Patchwork' hanging of Brighton on the facing page was later created and televised, resulting in a large increase in membership.

To Catrin

On the occasion of our 10th Birthday. From Sussex Quillers

Wi

Sheila Wyatt

Ann Bradley

23/7/90

We had a very successful and enjoyable event. Will send you a photo later on.

Wi.

Shena Wyatt   Ann Mar

Ann Bradley   Frances Thorne

Gill Caverly   From Gran
Ray Weeding   Sheila Smith
Audrey Benson   Gay Courtage
                     Nora Davies.

Doreen S. Megginson
Ruth Patys Fred Barfoot

Chris Rolfe
                     Margaret 3. machean
Sheila Baillie

18

CORNWALL

PART TWO
1985-1997

An enchanting county on the other side of the River Tamar
separating Cornwall from the rest of the country and
mostly observed and created in Textile Art

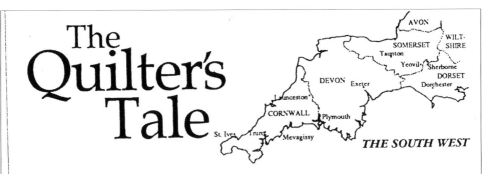

The Quilter's Tale

THE SOUTH WEST

(Map showing AVON, SOMERSET, WILTSHIRE, DEVON, DORSET, CORNWALL with towns: Taunton, Yeovil, Sherborne, Dorchester, Exeter, Launceston, St Ives, Truro, Mevagissy, Plymouth)

THE INDEPENDENT PATCHWORKER

St. Ives School of Painting, detail from Catrin Edwards-Jones applique wall hanging "A Peep at St. Ives"

Celtic Heritage

Catrin Edwards-Jones teaches textile art at the St. Ives School of Painting

painting on to silks, transfer printing on to textiles, batik and resist painting on to textiles.

Catrin is currently researching Celtic Art and has started a Celtic Heritage Workshop. Her students are using natural materials and natural dyes obtained from plants from the Cornish hedgerows.

TRADITIONAL APPROACH

The St Ives Quilt Group was started by Catrin Edwards-Jones

members live in an area that has long attracted artists it is not surprising that they too have turned to their surroundings for inspiration. Catrin puts the work of the St Ives Quilters in context.

St Ives is divided into two distinct areas: Downalong and Upalong. Upalong is where the families connected with the tin mining industry lived, and Downalong where the fishermen lived and worked. This all began to change around the turn of the century, when the pilchards were no longer so plentiful, and the Cornish holiday became popular. Downalong today is an artists colony. The excellent light must have contributed a great deal to this development, as Downalong is almost completely surrounded by the sea. It is now dotted with galleries, workshops and studios, and is most conducive to all kinds of artistic activity. The famous – Barbara Hepworth, Bernard Leach, Ben Nicholson and Alfred Wallis, to name a few – lived and worked here in the past, and there are numerous artists and craftsmen working here today.

When the St Ives Quilters got together in 1986 one of the first things the group made was a hanging showing favourite local views – and it was clear that as a group we could not help but be inspired by the magic of our surroundings.

The St Ives Quilters' came into being after a slide-show given by Catrin at an hotel belonging to her good friend Marriette – 'to cheer up a cold February evening'. With snow on the ground, over fifty people arrived in good spirit – resulting in over ten enthusiastic ladies wishing to be members of a creative quilting group; to become – THE ST. IVES QUILTERS'

THE ST. IVES TIMES AND ECHO and HAYLE TIMES, 17th April, 1987

THE ST.IVES
TIMES & ECHO

St. Ives scenes in quilters' birthday wall-hanging

TWELVE talented women have got St. Ives sewn up — beautifully.

The St. Ives Quilters, whose ancient art has revived and flourished under the expertise of textile artist Catrin Edwards-Jones, celebrated their first birthday at the Chy-an-Dour Hotel on Wednesday.

And it was a stylish occasion. Especially when the wraps were removed from their first year's labours, and a quilted applique wall-hanging depicting the many faces of St. Ives, was revealed in all its splendour.

The large hanging comprises sixteen original quilted blocks — each as individual as its creator — and highlighting a variety of scenes and situations in St. Ives.

For originality the Quilters deserve top marks. The overall effect of the finished item which is incorporated on a sea-scape background of bluey hues is stunning.

Their own description of the quilt as a "rag-bag hanging" does not do this commendable piece of work justice. Some of the blocks have been worked with the aid of original drawings and photographs whilst others depict scenes and sights captured through the windows of the Quilters homes.

The hanging has been created by: Margaret Polley (fisherman's cottage and Hepworth sculpture); Elaine Welch (Island Chapel by night and St. Ives fishing boats); Catrin Edwards-Jones (Smeaton's lighthouse); Mariette Triffit (Godrevy lighthouse and wind and shine); Lesley Ward (harbour and St. Ives School of Painting); Suzanne Newton (Knill's monument); Diane Sullivan (Sloop Inn); Celia Orchard (Wills Lane Gallery); Hilda Musitano (harbour and church and harbour and fishermen); Anne Macrae (Doll's House, Porthmeor Square), and "Mac" McAlindon (cats).

The end product belies the fact that many of the contributors were novices at the start.

In a year they have produced an exquisite item which captures the essential timelessness of St. Ives and which is destined to become an heirloom.

ST. IVES QUILTERS FIRST BIRTHDAY

THE St. Ives Quilters who celebrated their birthday at the Chy an Dour Hotel as reported last week.

THE ST. IVES' QUILTERS BLOCK QUILTED
PATCHWORK HANGING

Enlarged examples of a few very Cornish local scenes within the St. Ives hanging that won first prize at the Quilter's Guild annual A.G.M. meeting in Devon, under their competition title 'Sea Hangings'.

FACING PAGE TOP LEFT:
'Sweet Promise' a local fishing boat
– machine quilted applique by Elaine Welch

FACING PAGE TOP RIGHT:
St Ives 'Smeaton Pier'
– applique and machine quilted by Lesley Ward

FACING PAGE CENTRE LEFT:
A local interior, with a Cornish Pasty on the table
– by Margaret Polly

FACING PAGE CENTRE RIGHT:
The Godrevy Lighthouse
– by Marrietta Triffitt
– with rocks created from her husband's discarded tie

FACING PAGE BELOW:
St. Ives' Bay – two local fishermen and their boat
– textured applied appliqued batik
– by Hilda Musitano

FACING PAGE:
– reversible double-sided coverette
made of individual puffed squares

31

33

Batik work
exhibition

An exhibition of batik work was held at the St. Ives School of Painting to accompany the last Artists Lunch of the winter season.

Classes in batik were started by Catrin Edwards Jones and the group explored wax and paste resist textile techniques, using various dyes, experimenting with colour and 'resist' methods on the natural fibres of linen, silk and cotton.

Ideas were generated from drawings, sketches, photographs and lines from the poets. 'Enter these enchanted woods, you who dare', transferred well to good visual representation. The methods employed in batik lend themselves to forests, trees, landscape, the sea, and abstract subjects worked purely for the effect of colour tones and shapes.

The successful accomplishments of the group were evident in the work, and by confirmation from the numbers of people who commented on its excellence and how it was suitably mounted, displayed and hung.

The exhibition deserves to be shown in further venues and to this end Studio 7, in Bunkers Hill will be choosing and framing the best pieces for sale at the Easter opening.

Because of the interest shown in learning to work in batik an extra class will be run on Monday evening at the School of Painting, as well as the afternoon group. Both classes will start in the next winter term.   **M.W.**

FACING PAGE:
Activities on Porthmeor Beach, St. Ives
– quilted batik on cotton and applique

FACING PAGE:
Two local fishing boats
– machine embroidered batik, applique and textured embroidery

41

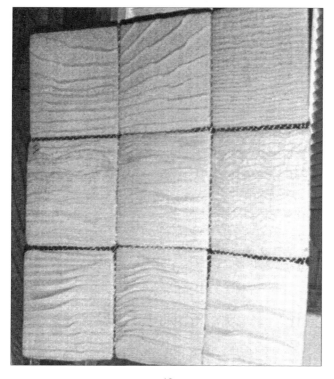

FACING PAGE:
Sun Set
– painting

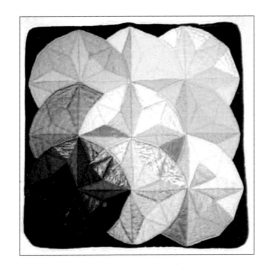

FACING PAGE ABOVE:
Sea and Sky
– transfer printing,
textured quilting and embroidery

FACING PAGE BELOW:
The Last Race
– oil painting

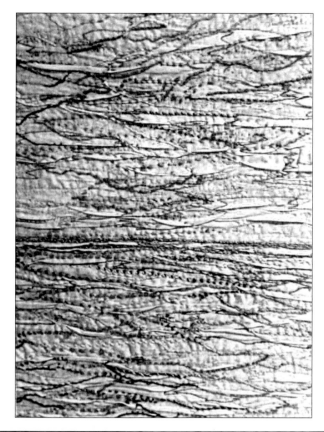

Three Hand-Made Boxes

FACING PAGE ABOVE:
– hand quilted lid

FACING PAGE CENTRE:
– transfer painted lid
machine quilted

FACING PAGE BELOW:
– canvas embroidered work box

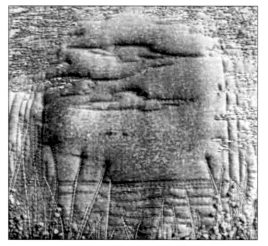

75

Dearest Cassim,

Saying "au revoir", sadly, opens the memory gates to those stimulating days in St Ives, when love of textiles and your creative skills inspired a wonderful atmosphere of work & play!

It remains with us, and I can only say thank you for sharing a very enjoyable slice of Life!

21 July '86

With all good wishes, Love, Margaret' x

With all my love to you both. I hope you will be happy in your new home. Jenny

Love and much happiness in your new venture Audrey/x

Hope & Best wishes for Lesley x

See you soon, Nanette

From St. Ives Quilters wishing you much happiness & peace in your new haven. Leaving us with many happy memories of ten years of your inspiration, enthusiasm & companionship. We shall miss you.

Best wishes for your new home Valerie.

With love & best wishes for the future Pat x

With love from Gladys

Hope you'll be very happy. With love & prayers Barbara x

78

Members of the St. Ives' Quilters' socialising

SUSSEX

PART THREE
1997-2005

Art examples carried out by Catrin on
her return from Cornwall to East Sussex
in
Textile Art, Ink and Wash, Watercolour
and Stained Glass

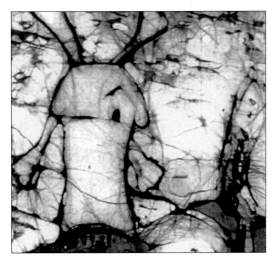

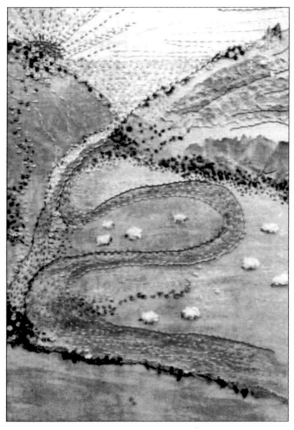

91

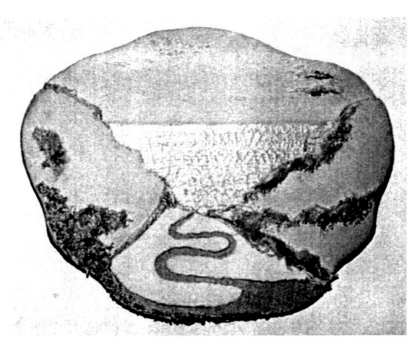

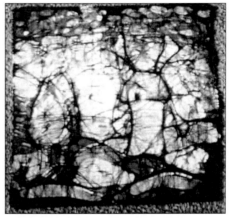

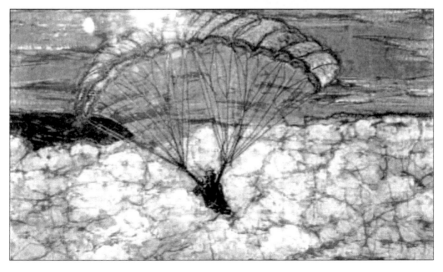

FACING PAGE ABOVE:
Saltdean Undercliff before snow storm
– oil painting

FACING PAGE BELOW:
'Rough Seas'
– batik quilted on silk
Catrin Edwards-Jones
(exhibited at Foyle's textile exhibition 1989)

101

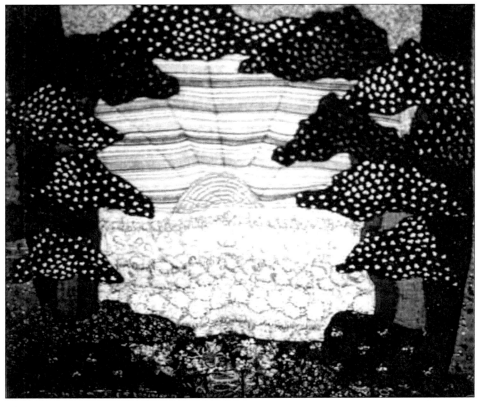

FACING PAGE ABOVE:
Sailing
– stained glass window

FACING PAGE BELOW:
Sailing
– pointillism on paper

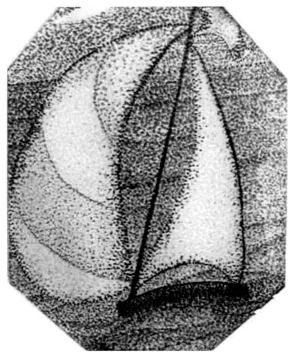

FACING PAGE ABOVE:
Transfer painting
– onto cotton

FACING PAGE BELOW:
Owls
– a mirror
stained glass

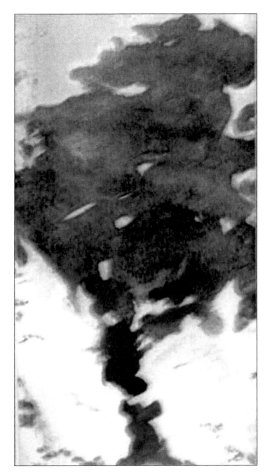

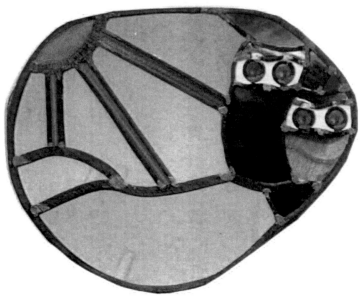

111

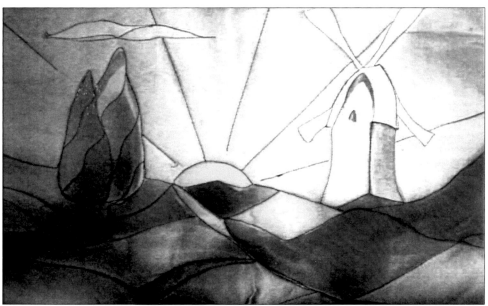

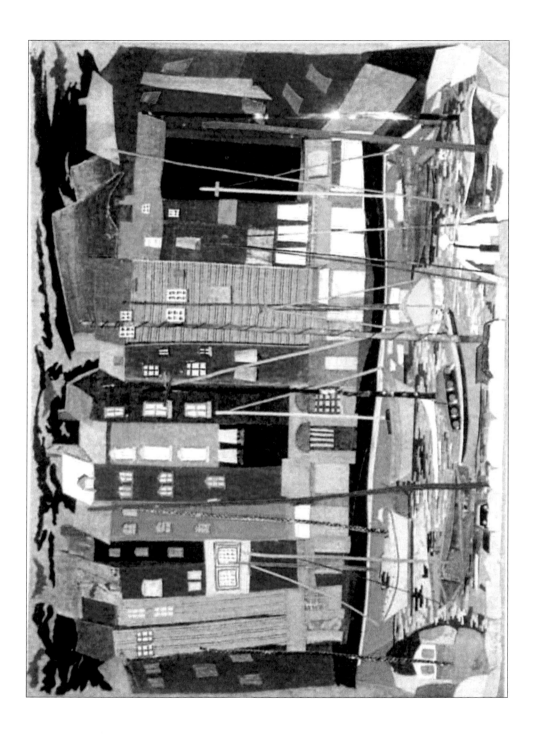

FACING PAGE ABOVE:
Entrance to Brighton Marina
– a cartoon
(for a stained glass window)

FACING PAGE BELOW:
Entrance to Brighton Marina
– stained glass window
Catrin Edwards-Jones

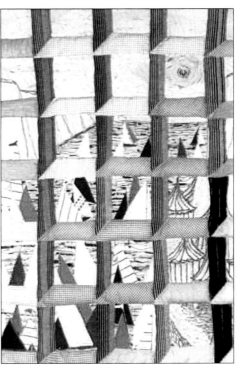

121

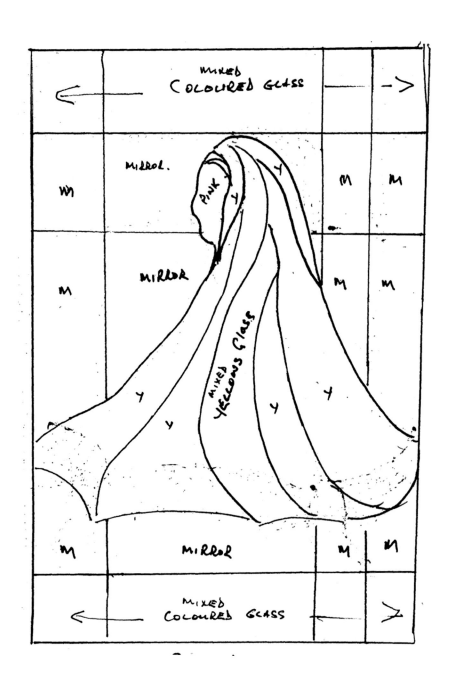

THE ALEX MIRROR

ABOVE: The preparation for the window

FACING PAGE: stained glass window

GLOSSARY

APPLIQUE Altering the surface by sewing one fabric over another. As a companion to patchwork and quilting; they go very well together.

INK and WASH WATERCOLOUR. Damp the paper before commencing.

PATCHWORK Making a quilt is in the form of three layers –
The top layer of a pieced design. The middle layer of wadding. The bottom layer of fabric. Quilted by hand or machine. The making of a larger design by repeating a pattern in different coloured, plain and patterned fabrics.

Old examples of patchwork have been found throughout history; some of the earliest in the Egyptian tombs. Early pilgrims took the craft to America during America's period of great depression. Their quilts were made from their favourite worn pieces of material – old patterned shirts and dresses. Various examples of quilts were created in America – Log Cabin. Tumbling Block, Crazy Patchwork, Block Patchwork and Wedding Ring, to mention but a few. Many families put aside their completed quilt in the bottom drawer of a dresser for their future brides-to-be.

QUILTING
Small running stitches through a top layer of fabric, middle wadding and a base cloth when worked by hand, or quilted by machine.

THE SUSSEX QUILTERS
In the 1950's at the 'Friends House' just off Brighton's Lanes in the centre of

the city, a meeting was held for a talk on new and old quilts. Catrin Edwards-Jones formed the Sussex Quilters on the occasion and about a dozen of the ladies present became the first members of the Sussex Quilters, followed by classes and fairs. A hanging of Brighton and some of the surrounding areas was to follow. A television crew arrived to record some of the work being carried out when in the making and completed for their final television programme. Due to many more members wishing to join the Sussex Quilters, all future meetings were held in a more convenient hall outside Brighton, in Southwick where the members are still creating quilts to this day.

ST. IVES QUILTERS
Formed by Catrin in 1986, following her slide talk at a St Ives' hotel on a cold winter's day. The new quilting group won first prize at the Quilters' Guild's annual A.G.M. held in Devon a year later, with their hanging of St. Ives. Catrin worked with the quilters over a period of ten years; resulting in all the members producing beautiful examples of Batik and Transfer Painting.

THE TATE GALLERY ON PORTHMEOR BEACH, ST. IVES
A large hanging portraying many activities on Porthmeor beach; worked in Batik (on an old cotton sheet for absorbance), quilted and appliqued. A hanging of the Tate Gallery, the Island Chapel, Artist quarters and the Surf School by Catrin.

TRANSFER PAINTING on TEXTILE
Drawing and Painting an image, in reverse, on paper. Place the paper on the cotton fabric and transfer the image onto the fabric with the aid of a hot smoothing iron.

WATER COLOUR – WAX RESIST. Pencil onto paper your subject; apply wax onto the areas to be highlighted before completing the watercolour in colour.